Water Buffaloes, Swim Holes, and Monkey Wallahs

Water Buffaloes, Swim Holes, and Monkey Wallahs

SNAPSHOTS FROM AN
AMERICAN TEENAGER IN PAKISTAN

BY STEFAN BORGES

Printed in the United States of America

Cover and interior designed by Megan Katsenavakis

Library of Congress Control Number: 2021910865
ISBN: 978-1-951568-15-3

SMALL
BATCH
BOOKS

493 SOUTH PLEASANT STREET
AMHERST, MASSACHUSETTS 01002
413.230.3943

SMALLBATCHBOOKS.COM

In memory of my dad, my mom,
and my brother, Michael

Contents

Preface

MY PARENTS FLED EAST GERMANY in 1953 and made their way to Chicago after the end of my father's work assignment in Colombia. Our first house in the U.S., a small two-bedroom one, was in Lombard, Illinois, and I attended grade school there. Due to my father's work as a civil engineer for Harza Engineering Company, we relocated overseas in 1968 to Pakistan for one of the projects. I attended an American international school (Lahore American School) in Lahore from junior high through high school, with classes based on the American system. This was a small private school for Americans, other foreign families from several countries, and wealthier Pakistani students. Once you graduate, all your credits applied to enter college stateside. I had a good experience at the school, and it helped that we stayed in one spot, so I could graduate from the same school.

This book is not about school, however; it's mostly about my experiences living in Pakistan between 1968 and 1973 as a teenager. I have been telling some of these stories over the years and began writing them down about ten years ago to share with others. Now that I am recently retired, it's a good time to tackle writing a book.

My interest in photography as a casual hobby began in school, mainly since there were plenty of interesting images to capture, from both living in this exotic country and traveling during home-leave trips.

My love of travel grew from the experiences of seeing other cultures, meeting people, and participating in various activities. I am thankful to my father for providing me these opportunities. His memoirs (*Five Countries*, by Alexander Borges), covering his life over several decades, constitute a more epic book, but this short book spans a period of about six years, a unique time period during our overseas life in Pakistan. This is a compilation of mini-stories and perspectives with photos that I took as a teenager. I hope the compilation provides some insight and amusement in embracing new roads and opportunities.

1

The Road to Lahore and New Beginnings

IN 1967, AT THE HEIGHT of the Cold War, I flew from Chicago to Germany as a twelve-year-old to spend the summer visiting relatives on both sides of the Wall. I stayed with my *oma* (grandma) in West Berlin. She spoke no English. I figured out later that my parents knew that my being with her would help my German. I understood the language but needed practice speaking it. Seven years earlier, I had learned English only after our family moved from Colombia to the U.S., when my father started working for Harza Engineering Company. (While in Germany, I missed my parents and friends back in Lombard, Illinois, since I'd never been away from them longer than ten days at summer camp in Wisconsin.)

My *oma* had a small apartment at the top of a three-story house in a nice suburb of West Berlin. She did not drive, so we walked everywhere, unless we took the *S-Bahn* into the city. I started making friends and getting comfortable finding things to do. I recall riding an old borrowed bike and being stopped by the German police for not following the rules; I was told to stay off the sidewalks or pay a fine. I understood exactly what they said, but I replied, "I'm from Chicago" and learned about the advantages of being multilingual. The reason I sometimes rode on the sidewalk was to avoid a few of the bumpy cobblestone streets. In the city center I recall a bike path between the sidewalk and the street, which I thought was a clever idea. On one of the walks with my *oma* along the park paths, I had brought my swimsuit, and I swam across a small pond and back—just to impress her, perhaps.

West Berlin was an island of freedom surrounded by communist East Germany. Witnessing the stark difference as I crossed the border via Checkpoint Charlie to visit my cousins shaped my perspective of the realities of the world. My *oma* stood on the west side and could only wave to her son (my uncle) and grandson (my cousin), who were standing fifty yards away on the east side, past the barbed wire, gates, and armed watchtower. Writing this was difficult, since I can still see her tears from not being able to hug her son and grandson. With an American passport, though, I could cross the border.

I understood clearly why my parents had fled East Germany, and I appreciated the opportunities that America gave us after having arrived from Colombia as a four-year-old.

Meanwhile, back in Illinois, my parents were moving from the Lombard two-bedroom house into a new house in the neighboring suburb of Glen Ellyn. Fortunately, they let me know about this before my trip. Little did they know that all their efforts of the move and of growing a new lawn would be passed on to the next owners eight months later.

I began seventh grade in a new town and neighborhood that had names for each model house. For some reason I had been more comfortable exploring West Berlin with newly made friends than I was trying to fit into a new large school in Glen Ellyn, where I felt I was just a number. Maybe my discomfort was from trying to adjust to junior high.

By Christmas, my father announced that we were moving to Pakistan and asked if we were okay with it. He had some big dam projects to work on for Harza. I immediately was excited for the complete change and the adventure. I pictured Timbuktu, camels, and people with long, loose clothing, just like in the movies. We prepared for the big move by getting the long list of vaccine shots over several doctor's visits; sorting our stuff by sea freight, air freight, and carry-on luggage; and spending hours taping music onto reel-to-reel tape, since we would not have AM/FM radio, and rock and jazz records would not be available during those days in Pakistan.

In February we flew out of O'Hare International. After a stop in Berlin to see *Oma* and make several more visits through Checkpoint Charlie to visit my aunt, uncle, and cousins, we continued on to Pakistan with one stop in Baghdad. Looking out the window on the Baghdad tarmac during refueling, I saw palm trees and my first camels. The boring school in Glen Ellyn, with its crowded classes, was a distant memory. New adventures were just beginning.

When we arrived at the small airport in Lahore, Pakistan, the welcome reception from my father's work associates, the flowered leis, and the unusual new sights and sounds were my first glimpses of my next two years, based on my father's initial contract.

Although I started at LAS (Lahore American School, a private American international school) in only the last few months of my seventh-grade year, it seemed like an easy transition. We immediately met families that worked with my father, and we met their friends. The classes were small. The average grade had from twenty to thirty students each, depending on the year. Everything was casual and more relaxed. The next social party was always being planned. We soon learned that my father's contract would be extended, so Lahore became my home for five and a half years. By high school, I really got into my comfort zone, and I felt lucky to finish graduation at the same school.

Although it was a small school, it offered any number of school activities, sports, and social events both around town and in the region. The school had been converted from an old mansion right across from the canal. When the water flowed, water buffaloes would be bathing in the canal, just downstream from where some people were washing their clothes.

2

Housing, Kitchens, and Such

AFTER ARRIVING IN PAKISTAN IN 1968, when I was a thirteen-year-old, we moved into our temporary housing in WAPDA flats,[1] until we were able to select a house to move into. Not much can be said about the flats; we're typically not apartment dwellers. The antique elevators had the classic folding-cage door, and it seemed like it took forever to go up and down in the three-story building. You were grateful when the door finally opened.

But it didn't matter, since we soon moved into our first house. However, we had our eye on another house, which was under construction by a Pakistani engineer who had studied architecture in Canada, and after a few short months, that house would become our home for the next five years.

---

1   WAPDA stands for Water and Power Development Authority, the client of Harza Engineering Company.

The first house was in an older suburban neighborhood. Not only did each bedroom have its own bathroom, but each bathroom on the first floor had a second door with access to the outside. That's because it was the job of the outdoor sweeper to clean the bathroom.

My mom had the duty of interviewing all the candidates for the various servant positions. Servants loved working for Americans, who paid very well. As soon as any foreigner arrived in Lahore, servants began showing up at the doorstep with reference letters in hand; they were vying for the most sought-after positions: the cook, followed by the indoor housekeeper, the driver, and then the gardener. Books can be written about the hiring and firing of servants. A lot of guidance was provided by the American Women's Club. Suffice it to say that we learned it was more important to hire a cook who is trustworthy, shows up for work, fits with the personality of the family, and can learn to cook, rather than just hire someone who can cook.

Anyway, Americans, especially young teenagers, are used to popping into the kitchen to see what food is available. So on one of my first visits into the kitchen, I saw something big lying on the counter, and it wasn't a cut of beef or chicken. I was getting a little concerned, and I asked what it was.

"Master Sab, this is ox tongue."

I suggested to my mom that I never wanted to see that again in our kitchen. Now, in fairness to the food critics who say I should at least have tried ox tongue, I apparently had eaten it in a previous meal, when I hadn't known what it was, and I had not cared for it.

The only other wonderful moment in the first house was the Christmas-like joy of unpacking the sea freight that had just arrived after its three-month journey over the high seas, the Karachi port, and then via truck to Lahore. My blue ten-speed Schwinn bike arrived in one piece.

Shortly afterward, the new house was ready. The architecture was a fusion of practical Pakistani suburban house design with a sort of modern California touch. A hallway wrapped around a beautiful outdoor atrium and led to most of the bedrooms and the kitchen. It was a single story, except for one room on the second floor near the entrance, which was the library, where the owner kept all his engineering books.

Our home had the typical flat roof, except over the library, where the curved roof gave a distinct feature for the front of the house. By the way, from the point of view of an eighth-grader, all the homes in Lahore were excellent for climbing onto the roofs, one of the favorite pastimes of us teenagers and great for launching sky rockets or for flying kites.

The floors included inlaid marble. The owner even had a built-in desert cooler (a fan blowing air over water). Of course, we installed an air conditioner in each room for the 100°F–115°F dry-heat days.

One night I ventured into the dark kitchen to see what was in the fridge, or to get another bottle of treated water. I heard some crunching sounds under my feet. I'm trying to recall if I was wearing sandals. Yes, I must have worn sandals. I turned on the lights and discovered that I had just stepped on some cockroaches. The others scurried off. I'm sure the cook must have later gotten rid of them, but in any event, every time I entered the kitchen in the evening after that experience, I first turned on the lights. And every evening from then on, one of the duties of the cook was to leave a cold bottle of water on the nightstands in our bedrooms. Other friendly visitors to our house were small green geckos. When I first tried to catch one off the ceiling, I was surprised when its tail fell off. Their tails grew back, but from then on, I just let them be.

Life was good! Daily life in Lahore itself was an adventure, and it helped to have a sense of humor.

Our house in Lahore.

Our gardener with his family.

A new house going up next to ours.

Mom, behind the wheel of our VW, during a shopping trip in Lahore.

3

A Trip to Swat and Walking on Ice

IN THE SUMMER OF 1969, our family took a trip from Lahore up to Swat, in northern Pakistan. We had a Land Rover with a driver, and we made stops along the way—including Mangla Dam, a favorite stop, since my father had previously worked on the design of the spillway while still in Chicago.

To get to Swat, you continue driving past Islamabad, past the Indus River (site of the next big dam, Tarbela), and on to Peshawar. From there you head north to Swat. It was a long drive, with the land and climate changing from arid to valleys lush from the mountain waters. Off in the distance we noticed a caravan of nomads moving across a valley.

Along the way we stayed at a small hotel (more like a rest house) run by a retired British officer. The hotel was clean, and the food reflected the simplicity of British cuisine. Compensating for the blandness of the food was the conversation with the officer. I pictured stories from Rudyard Kipling.

On one of our stops along the mountain road, we got out of the vehicle for a view of the Swat River. After missing Chicago winters, we were amazed to once again see some snow and ice over a portion of the rushing river below and up on the mountaintops.

As our parents watched from the road, my brother, Michael, and I climbed down the rocks to pick up some snow. An ice bridge spanned the river, and we wanted to stand on the ice near the bank. We looked up at our parents and saw them waving to us with what seemed like much enthusiasm, but we could not hear them due to the thundering river. So we waved back. After we returned to the Land Rover, we saw that our father was not happy. He said he'd been trying to get our attention after he saw the middle of the ice bridge collapse into the river. He'd been very concerned that we would try to walk too far out on the ice, although we had no intention of doing that. Looking back at it now as a parent, I completely understand his concern.

Some German friends had joined us in Swat, and the two Land Rovers drove as far as the road would take us. Then we had a picnic in a meadow area with small creeks to cool our feet. I recall that the water was ice cold. We breathed in the clean air and enjoyed the aroma of pine as though we were in the Alps. Our friends wanted to toast the moment, but someone forgot the bottle opener. One of our friends impressed us by using a key to pop the cap off the beer bottle, and we then enjoyed our lunch. Afterward, we began the drive back along the narrow mountain road through the Swat Valley and eventually to Lahore. When we learned that my father's contract would be extended, we were happy that we could take many more regional trips over the next four years.

The family cools off in a stream in Swat.

4

The President Visits Lahore

WHEN THE NEWS CAME IN that the president of the United States would visit Lahore in 1969, it was a big deal for everyone. A few days prior to President Nixon's arrival, the main tree-lined boulevard from the airport into the city, which passed by the hotels and consulates, had its lines and curbs freshly painted.

From the point of view of an American living overseas in the late 1960s, as much as the adventures and the new experiences were exciting, we were all feeling very far from home and our country. So getting the latest records by our favorite rock band, getting a few commissary foods to supplement the pantry and the local groceries, and having our president fly into our small airport was exciting stuff. On the international scene, President Nixon was well respected. Domestic political problems were still in their early stages, and anyway, that is not what this story is about.

I recall that the weather was already very hot, so I am sure the visit was sometime in July or August. During the summer in Lahore, the big problem is finding something to do, since many of our friends took yearly home-leave trips then. Having such a big event gave us plenty to talk about as we looked forward to the chance of seeing our president.

The day arrived for the big visit, so everyone headed to the airport. My parents, my four-year-old sister, Beatrice, and I got a great spot right next to the four-foot-high chain-link fence by the tarmac. The crowd grew with Americans, other Westerners, local dignitaries, and reporters. Now came the big wait and the anticipation.

Finally, two Boeing 707s arrived: Air Force One and a second plane just to carry all the reporters. The stairs were rolled up to the plane, the red carpet rolled out, and probably a band was getting ready (I don't recall exactly, but that would have been expected). Finally, the door opened, and our president was now waving to the crowd. What a proud moment!

As a young, skinny but fast-growing teenager, I felt the over-$100°F$ heat starting to get to me, and my head was getting dizzy. Apparently, I should have been drinking some water or Coke, but I didn't. So now I had to find a place away from the crowd and sit down.

My parents and sister still held their prime spot when the president made his way along the fence. My father held Beatrice up by the fence, and now we have a photo of her reaching out and touching his face. Meanwhile, I was sitting on a curb by the front door of the airport, resting and lamenting that I was missing everything by the fence. Well, suddenly the black limos began leaving the airport, driving by slowly, right in front of me. And there, five feet away, sat President Nixon, looking out the window and waving back.

It was interesting to read in the papers the news of the American president traveling around the world, but his visit to Lahore was an experience I'll always remember. There were many stories that center around the airport, and this was only one of them.

5

Home Leave 1970:
Trip Around the World, Going East

IN 1970 WE HAD OUR first home-leave trip from Pakistan, and since my father's contract had been extended, it would be a round trip heading east until we returned to Lahore at the end of the summer. My father scheduled the trip so that we could see some highlights in different cities for three days or so each and then take a relaxing break by the beach in between for a week or two at a time.

After Bangkok, Hong Kong, Kyoto, and Tokyo, we spent five days at a beach house in Hawaii. I still recall the song I heard when I turned on the FM station in the rental car: "Spill the Wine," by Eric Burdon and War. Then off to L.A. and then Puerto Vallarta for another relaxing five days on the beach. By this time it was June, and we noticed what looked like athletes and their beautiful wives at the poolside. It turned out they were Dallas Cowboys players on vacation before the practice season started. One was wearing a cast on his arm.

Then it was off to Mexico City to see my father's cousin and family. We were there during a World Cup soccer match between Brazil and Germany, so while everyone was watching the games on TV, we visited the pyramids without crowds. In Chicago we visited my uncle's family and friends, and we did some shopping. I'm sure my father checked in at Harza's offices in the city.

Next was London, followed by Germany, where my father purchased a VW fastback to ship back to Lahore after we drove around Europe. We visited friends and relatives in Germany, including visits again in West and East Berlin. Then we drove south to Munich, Salzburg in Austria, and on to Yugoslavia, to spend two weeks on the Adriatic coast.

My father returned to Pakistan to work, and my mom, my sister, and I drove back to Germany to ship the car to Lahore. With replenished supplies of records and tapes, new jeans, and gym shoes, we headed back to Pakistan.

It was a grand trip, and I was old enough to appreciate it.

During 1970 it was the height of the Vietnam War, and I noticed American servicemen taking R&R weekend trips in Hong Kong, and they did not waste their time as they made the most of their short break from the war. As we passed through the airport in Hawaii, we saw many young soldiers with their duffel bags heading to Vietnam. This was another reality check—besides reading about the war in the papers.

Over the decades things have changed quite a bit. Places I visited later were not as safe, and places we avoided, such as Vietnam and Laos, are now tourist destinations. It goes to show you that when you have the opportunity to travel to certain countries, take advantage of it, since things could change down the road.

6

Swimming in Pakistan

IN 1968, SHORTLY AFTER MOVING to Lahore, we discovered several nice pools, including popular ones at the Ambassador Hotel and the Intercontinental Hotel. Eventually, an American club opened up, also with a clean and refreshing pool. We preferred the Punjab Club next to the polo fields, with the old-world charm of its billiard room and its open membership for our friends with various citizenships.

Our school, LAS, had originally been an old mansion, and it had a small built-in pool, about fifteen meters long. It was a few steps above the outdoor basketball court. Our swim team used it for practice, but the lanes were too short. By eighth grade I found myself in local swim meets representing LAS, and sometimes our names got in the sports section of the *Pakistan Times*. Events were sponsored by the Pakistan Swimming Federation.

A local college hosted many of the swim events, since they had a twenty-five-meter pool, but unfortunately, their filter system was not maintained, so often this pool was green. When we arrived at the meets, our biggest fear was getting an ear infection. We jumped in only at race time and then had an incentive to swim as quickly as possible so we wouldn't catch anything. Due to poor visibility, we had to be careful when turning at the walls.

The following year I swam in more meets. My brother, Michael, also swam and did especially well in the long-distance events. One day our office at LAS received a letter from the Central Zone Swim Association inviting Michael and me to join swimmers from various schools in the Punjab region to compete in the nationals in Karachi. We were surprised, and we were the only foreigners going at that time. We had accepted the honor and agreed to attend, although we preferred to make our own travel arrangements (with the help of our dad) to fly down to Karachi and stay at the Intercontinental Hotel. The other swimmers went by third-class train and had other accommodations, so we didn't really get to know the rest of the team.

On the first day of the meet, we walked into a modern-looking university campus with a beautiful full-size pool filled with crystal-clear water. I was impressed.

We placed in the first couple of heats and felt good about advancing to the finals. Then a dispute began about the finishing times of a few of our swimmers, with our coach claiming foul play. It appeared that decisions leaned heavily in favor of another region. After that first day, our coach pulled the Punjab team out of the meet in protest, and we all went home. This was disappointing.

Upon arriving home at the airport in Lahore, we found to our surprise a group of family and LAS supporters greeting us; they were unaware that we had swum only the one day. In the end it didn't matter much to anyone. I think they cheered us on because we had gone to a national meet. I also thought that if you wanted an easier path to participate in the Olympics, you could try joining a national team of a small country that was still developing a sport.

I swam decently enough, but then a new swimmer arrived from the States who was now the fastest sprinter and starter and who could do the fastest turns. It was evident that he had extensive training. From my understanding, back in the States, prior to his family's move to Pakistan, he had been on track to qualify for the Olympics.

After graduating from a class of nine people, I returned to the States to attend Northern Illinois University (NIU), a school of about twenty-four thousand students in the cornfields of Illinois. I walked into the field house before classes began and looked for the swim coach. I introduced myself and said I had just arrived from Lahore and would like to join the swim team that was listed in the NIU brochure. He did not know anything about Pakistan, but he said, "Sure. Just show up to practice in the morning."

I quickly learned about serious swim practices several hours a day, and my swimming improved. But I knew it would take a year or two to get to the level of the other swimmers, who had already had years of heavy training. I also discovered that the water polo team was an extension of the swim team and that they needed another player. With my basketball background, it was an easy transition to water polo. Swim practices and playing water polo for two years with matches against schools such as the University of Wisconsin, Lake Forest College, and Northwestern in Chicago improved my swimming.

Due to early-morning and afternoon practices, I enjoyed a side benefit of getting a single room in a dormitory at the center of campus, very close to the pool. That is when I met Nancy, my future wife. In hindsight, I see that swimming contributed to my meeting her and in building a wonderful family life after college.

7

From Ten-Speed Bike to Motorbike

MY FATHER ESPECIALLY ENJOYED RECALLING this story, about how I got the okay to get a motorbike.

From seventh grade through ninth grade, my normal modes of transportation included taking taxis and rickshaws, getting rides from other people, riding my forty-dollar used ten-speed Schwinn bike, and occasionally having my parents drop me off somewhere or having our cook, Solomon, drive us. I once commented to my dad that it was crazy to ride a motorbike or scooter in Pakistan with its busy traffic, dodging bikes, horse-drawn carts, rickshaws, double-decker buses, and scooters.

By high school I began golfing at the Pakistan Western Railways (PWR) golf club, northward down the street, along the canal past our school and along the train tracks. Often my father would drive me to the golf course, perhaps a twenty-minute ride.

Then one day I said, "Dad, if I had a small motorbike, I could take myself to the golf course, and it would be much more practical." I also pointed out that I would be careful. After all, I was already riding on the same roads on my ten-speed. A short time later, I was riding a brand-new red Honda 70 cc. (In later years I learned that my father had had a motorbike as a teenager in Germany before World War II, so he could probably relate to my enthusiasm.)

By this time in early high school, I already had reached my height of about six feet two inches, so my sitting on this small bike was noticeable. But I didn't care, since I had a certain sense of freedom, and it was an easy bike to learn on. There was still an issue with carrying a golf bag on the bike, though, so I learned that if I joined the PWR golf club, I would get a locker, and I mentioned that to my dad. Upon reflection, I guess this motorbike thing turned into a golf membership. Of course, everything there was relatively affordable compared to stateside. At least it was not the more expensive Gymkhana Golf Course.

The PWR golf club, by the way, was along the train tracks. I noticed some mud huts across the tracks and women making cakes of buffalo dung to dry on the stone beds along the tracks—cakes to be used for fuel for cooking or heating their mud huts in the winter. Also, a camel pulled a roller that would trim the fairway grass.

Many of us preferred this course, since it was very casual and relaxed, besides being affordable. Occasionally, the golf caddies would show off their skill and hit a few balls. They were quite good and gained instant respect.

Looking back at it, I realize that some would say I may have been spoiled. But these are deserved compensations for spending every other summer in Lahore in the heat while many friends were on summer home-leave trips or returning to the States. Golf and swimming were good ways to make use of the time.

I think everyone agreed, including my friends with motorbikes, that I needed to upgrade. A friend who was moving had a Honda 125 cc bike and offered to sell it to me for $400, which was about the same amount I got from selling my one-year-old Honda 70 cc. In the summer of '72, I had a great backpack trip through Europe and a home-leave trip to the States, and when I returned to Lahore in August for my senior year, my Honda 125 was waiting for me.

Several of my LAS friends had motorbikes. It was a great way to get around town to see friends and to get home from basketball practice after school. I took my camera to explore more places and take advantage of all the sights and experiences before moving back to the States after graduation. Incidentally, I think the money from selling the Honda 125 before going to college was spent on my trip through Europe on my way back to the States.

Farmers near Lahore.

A water buffalo enjoying some shade.

Farmers on a break.

Biking with friends by a village just outside Lahore.

My Honda 125 cc.

8

Permission to Get Towed

IN THE LATE '60S AND early '70s, American teenagers living in Pakistan had plenty of spare time and always looked for new activities. Just south of our neighborhood in Gulberg, Lahore, was a small airport. The land around the runway was a great playground, where we rode horses at full gallop, trying not to fall off. We also rode our bikes over pathways in some of the rough terrain.

The Walton Airport did not see much airplane activity, but my brother and I noticed one day that a single-engine plane was pulling a glider. Our father, always flexible with our ideas, helped inquire about our latest goal of taking a glider ride. We found out that a license was required to get lessons or a ride. Moreover, the Pakistan Civil Aviation Authority would not permit foreigners to fly from Walton Airport, since it was only fifteen miles from India, too close to the border.

Of course, that did not stop us from trying. We were told that we needed to go to Karachi in order to ride a glider. A Pakistani family friend knew someone at a small airport outside Karachi, and my father made the arrangements. We flew south on a Pakistan International Airlines jet, and our friends drove us out to the airport, which was a few miles inland from the Indian Ocean. There was plenty of wind along with updrafts from the heat, which made for ideal conditions for flying without an engine.

We arrived at the flight school and walked up to the glider. Now that I saw the bulky glider close up, I noticed that it looked a lot heavier and older than I had expected. It was not one of those newer, slick European sailplanes but was more like a vintage training glider from the 1940s.

The pilot sat in the front seat, and in a few minutes, we would be airborne, somehow. I asked where the other plane was, the one that would be towing us. Then, after the crew hooked the cable onto the glider, I noticed a jeep pull away, and we began moving. Soon we were off the ground. As we were gaining altitude and the jeep was nearing the end of the runway, the thought occurred to me how important it was that the cable would release properly. Then suddenly, we were free of the jeep, and we began circling in the updrafts. I remember seeing camels walking below and the expanse of the ocean nearby. The only sound was the wind, since we sat in an open cockpit—much like in the old biplanes, except we were without an engine and had only a single wing. After a short flight, we returned for a smooth landing. Walking away from the glider, I was amazed that it had ever got airborne. All in all, the mission was a success.

In 2011 I checked online and discovered that there is a gliding club website in Pakistan for paragliding, hang gliding, and motorized gliding. I guess, looking back forty years, I was on the ground floor of a future gliding club.

9

Dental Stories

A Low-Budget Dental Service

The wide gap between rich and poor in Pakistan was on constant display and not easy to ignore. Mixed in with the sights and sounds of the roadside vendors—the spicy aromas from the stalls selling meat dishes and the colorful fruit carts—you could discover almost any kind of service. You never knew what you would come across. Our family once noticed a makeshift dental service with a wooden chair and a box full of used teeth.

We didn't stay around to watch any procedures, but someone explained one to us. A client with a bad toothache would sit down and select a replacement tooth. The high back and roof over the seat was to keep the customer from jumping out of the chair while the bad tooth was pulled. I am not sure if this was a bit exaggerated, but it would explain the design of the chair. The tooth merchant would then file a groove on an adjoining tooth and then tie a string around the new tooth, which would hold it in place until the string fell off.

I would think the clients were required to pay in advance before the so-called dental procedure, and I'm not sure how much repeat business the vendor received. It's just another reminder of the tough circumstances that many people live in and to appreciate what we have.

A Wise Orthodontist

On the other end of the spectrum were the doctors, including orthodontists, that wealthier people could afford. I was talking to my father in 2014, when he was almost ninety-two years old, and the topic of Dr. Niazi, the orthodontist and dentist from Lahore, came up in conversation. My brother, Michael, had some work done by Dr. Niazi.

Dr. Niazi did good work, and one day he got a call from Prime Minister Zulfikar Ali Bhutto, who requested that he come to Islamabad and treat him. This call added to Dr. Niazi's reputation as a good orthodontist.

A few years later, Bhutto was arrested for political reasons in a military coup. After Bhutto was executed, Dr. Niazi fled Pakistan for his own safety to avoid being arrested, since he was known as being one of Bhutto's doctors and may have been considered a friend of his. That was probably a wise move by Dr. Niazi.

By the way, Bhutto's children attended the American school in Islamabad, and someone pointed them out while our basketball team visited for some tournament games. Little did we know at the time that many years later, Bhutto's daughter Benazir would one day become prime minister herself but would later be forced to go into exile. She would return in 2007 but would be assassinated after a couple of months.

10

Lahore to Kabul via the Khyber Pass

IN THE SUMMER OF '71, we had a family college friend from Munich staying with us in Lahore for a month or so. Our families were in the third generation of friendship, going back to when our grandparents had first met in the 1930s in Germany. Reiner, the college student, was quite intelligent, as we learned from playing card or board games with him during his visit. He could play two games of chess at the same time with my brother and myself, and he would always win. It was no surprise that he would end up having a successful career as a lawyer.

During his stay with us, we took a regional trip to Kabul. We were six people, and we had a VW fastback that sat only four comfortably. Since we all wanted to experience the drive along the route of Alexander the Great, my engineering father, Alexander, came up with the plan. My parents, Beatrice, and I would drive up to Kabul and meet Michael and Reiner, who would fly up. Then on the return, my mom and Beatrice would fly back to Lahore, and the guys would drive back through the Khyber Pass and on to Lahore. My dad and I would benefit by driving round trip.

On the way up, we did the usual stops, resting either in Rawalpindi (near Islamabad) or the Tarbela Dam site and then continuing to Peshawar by the Afghan border in the North-West Frontier Province.

On the morning that my dad drove us through the pass, we had heavy rains, and it was difficult to see which was the right road. My father stopped by a house where he saw people sitting on the veranda. With the window rolled down, he asked which way to the Khyber Pass. A woman sent out her older son, who then jumped on his motorbike and signaled us to follow.

After passing through a gate, we were now under the control of the Tribal Areas. Pakistan and the Tribal Areas in the North-West Frontier Province had an agreement: The tribes would guarantee the safety of travelers only if they stayed on the main road during the day. Off the road or at night, you took a risk. In hindsight, I realize that it was important to not run into mechanical problems and get stuck after hours.

At the Khyber Pass I still recall seeing the large concrete blockades scattered at the bottom of a gorge to prevent enemy tanks from driving through. Overloaded buses and Soviet-built cars drove along the pass; a typical sight was cars loaded with too many passengers. This was truly rugged country, and the road had multiple switchbacks and tunnels. Guardrails were few, and the drop-offs kept everyone on edge. Who needs thrill rides at amusement parks when you have the Khyber Pass to drive on?

Occasionally, we came across a small valley with a village or saw a mud fort strategically placed on a hilltop. We had a few tense moments navigating the flooded dry streambeds along the road, but we managed to make it through across the Afghan border.

Then off we went to Kabul. At the Intercontinental Hotel in Kabul, I noticed an American camper parked in front, and I asked the owners where they were from. The American family was traveling around the world and making purchases along the way for their boutique shop in Hawaii. I was impressed with their enterprising adventures.

We spent some days in Kabul, shopping and even visiting the residence of the American ambassador, Robert G. Neumann. We each had been hosts for our school-flag football teams (LAS and Kabul American School). His son had stayed at our house, and Michael had stayed at their residence.

After my mom and Beatrice flew back, we then drove to Lahore. On the open, flatter roads, Reiner drove the VW as though he were on the autobahn in Bavaria. At the border, however, my father took over the driving through the pass and back to left-hand driving.

I recall that we would occasionally see the so-called "hippies" making their way to India with stops in Lahore, where they would stay at some budget hotel in the older part of the city. They had quite a different experience from us foreigners living in comfort. Some of the hippies who traveled via the road from Europe would venture through the Khyber Pass, which was risky if they were not aware of the local rules—such as not traveling overnight.

This was another grand adventure of several trips we took while living in Pakistan. Looking back, I feel fortunate for these experiences, since things changed a few years later, and visiting these areas currently would be a bigger challenge. Years later, while watching the news during Operation Desert Storm, I recognized Mr. Neumann being interviewed as an expert on the Middle East and Afghanistan, and he would weigh in with his opinions.

*A tribal village stop with my brother, Michael; Reiner,
a friend from Germany; and my father.*

The road through the Khyber Pass.

A typical site on the Khyber Pass.

A fork in the road during our Khyber Pass trip.
(Camels to the right, cars to the left.)

Michael and Dad viewing Mangla Dam.

11

A "Three-Hour Tour" on the Mangla Dam Lake

PRIOR TO MOVING TO PAKISTAN, my father had already worked on one of the key elements of Mangla Dam: the design of its spectacular spillway. When we arrived at the dam, it was just like I had pictured it, having seen it on the cover of a magazine and on a stamp. The spillway was the prominent feature of the dam, along with the beautiful lake. (As a side note, dams and bridges are often featured on stamps, and that may be one of the reasons my father built an extensive collection of engineering-related stamps, which he entered into shows.)

Before our private tour of the dam, we stopped in at the Colony, with its curbs and paved streets, where many engineers and contractors had lived during construction. It looked like a transplanted subdivision from California or Arizona. After construction, only a few engineers had remained, and it now seemed like a ghost town. The

Colony also had the only bowling alley in Pakistan. If you bowled, a person would appear behind the pins after your turn and manually set them up again.

We drove along the road on the top of the dam over the spillway and to the ancient Mangla Fort, now an International Historical Heritage site. The engineering of the dam included a design to preserve the fort. The contrast between modern and ancient engineering was one of a kind.

On this particular trip, we met some friends, a German-American couple. They had brought their inflatable Zodiac-style boat, complete with a small motor. The plan was that while my father was busy meeting with one of the engineers, my mom, Beatrice, and I would join the couple on a short boat ride across Mangla Dam Lake.

The lake is about twenty-plus miles long, and the width where we crossed was about two to three miles. It was clear but dark, since the average depth was around two hundred feet. We were at the shore just past the powerhouse for the boat entry. Nearby I noticed a ferryboat that took locals to a small town somewhere along the length of the lake.

My father saw us off and agreed to meet us back at the beach after about three hours. Now we could see the dam from the lake's perspective. There were no other boats except that ferryboat in the far distance. What a perfect day!

We continued until we reached the other side and pulled into a small cove with barren hills as a backdrop. We saw another old fort perched on a hill. We tied down the boat and took a short hike up to explore the fort. We went back to the boat for our return trip and considered how lucky we were not only to enjoy this ride but to discover some history on our own.

The owner of the boat pulled the cord to start the engine, but it did not start. He tried several times. Nothing. We determined to go to plan B and row back. Rowing was very slow, since either there was only one oar or it just took forever with four adults in a rubber boat. We saw no other boats in the lake except the ferryboat in the distance, which was crossing at about the middle of the lake. I decided to take matters in my own hands: I jumped into the water, and using my frog kick, I pushed the boat about a mile so that we would be spotted by the ferryboat. I had to get used to the idea that I was swimming in very deep, very cold water.

Once we were in the middle, the ferryboat came close enough to see us waving and agreed to tow us in. My father had been waiting a long time and told us that he had been getting a little concerned. But then again, he was used to such minor misadventures on family outings. Although the motor had failed, our trip was a success.

Looking back now, I think that perhaps swimming in places such as Mangla Lake prepared me for some cold, open-water swims in Lake Michigan years later: the 2.5K swims at Navy Pier and then, when I was in my mid-fifties, 5K swims. The Chicago skyline views during the swim off Ohio Street Beach are much more urban in comparison to those of Mangla Lake.

*The view from Mangla Fort with the Mangla Dam spillway
in the background.*

12

Do You Trust Your Smuggler?

A FAMILY TRIP WITH A Land Rover and a driver who knew the territory was an ideal way to visit choice spots in the North-West Frontier Province. Each tribe or village specialized in a business and set the local rules.

One of our stops was in Derra, which was a gun-manufacturing town. Along our walk down the dirt main street, we saw various shops where craftsmen using manual tools made guns and rifles, including very good replicas. For example, you could buy a "Colt" revolver with a "Made in the USA" label. A vendor who heard you speak German would ask if you were interested in a "Mauser." The craftsmen even made some innovative James Bond–type walking canes and a "pen gun" that really did look like a heavy metal pen; only you didn't fill it with ink.

Smuggling was another big business, and Landhi Kotal was a

destination shopping town near the Khyber Pass where you could purchase imported goods duty-free in the good old days. Merchandise such as fabrics, electronics, and appliances would arrive in Karachi by ship, and then the goods would continue overland by truck to Afghanistan, just past the Pakistani border. The trucks would unload, and carriers would deliver the goods a few hundred yards back across the border into Pakistan's North-West Frontier Province. Hence, it was duty-free. Duty-free shopping in Amsterdam or in Hong Kong was based on a slightly different system.

Anyway, Landhi Kotal had many shops with goods spread out on tables under the awnings, and some larger shops you could walk through. My father recalled a Pathan shopkeeper saying that "our enemies we cut their throats, our friends we drink tea with." He asked my dad if he was a friend. Of course, my dad replied yes, and after tea they talked business.

My mom became an expert in shopping all over the world, and so we bought some items in Landhi Kotal. If you purchased just a few items, you would simply drive home after stopping at the checkpoint when leaving the Tribal Areas. Hopefully, you would avoid having to pay duties. If you purchased a larger amount, you could arrange for a 5-percent fee of the value of the goods to have them delivered to your hotel in Peshawar, across the border.

A German couple we knew made a large purchase and returned to their hotel and waited. That night no delivery was made. They waited until the next day, but the smugglers never arrived. Disappointed, our friends returned to Lahore, thinking they had learned an expensive lesson. To their surprise, about a week later, one of the smugglers showed up at their house in Lahore to explain that there had been problems at the border and to apologize for the loss of their goods. One of the messengers who had handled their goods had gone through the wrong border crossing and had been stopped by customs going into Pakistan.

However, in good faith, the smugglers made the effort to travel to Lahore and provide compensation equal to the value of the lost goods.

If you're a tribesman who builds a business and reputation on quality smuggling, then you can count on a deal with a handshake. It's all about honor.

So yes, you can trust your smuggler.

13

The *Chowkidar* (Night Watchman)

AS I RECALL THE EVENTS, it started with our discovering a six-inch cut on the metal screen by my bedroom window. We did not know who had done this, but it appeared to be a burglary attempt. We had all the normal security measures, including a six-foot-three-inch wall and a gated driveway. We added architectural metal grills over the windows and decided to hire a *chowkidar* (night watchman).

The search began, and in a short time, my father hired a Pathan. Although he was older, he was also very tall and looked like he would provide the security we needed. He came with an outstanding résumé; he had worked for one of the previous Harza managers whom he called "the general." He would mainly be available during the winter, since by summer he would go back up north.

One night we drove home in our VW fastback. We opened the big metal gates and drove onto our driveway until the headlights shone on our garage. In front of the garage door was our *chowkidar*, sitting on a chair fast asleep.

Having a night watchman falling asleep at night could be an issue. My father had a solution. He asked our *chowkidar* if he would like to make a little more money by washing our car. The only requirement was that the car would need to be washed at 2:00 a.m.

Our *chowkidar* was very enthusiastic for the added responsibility and the money. During one of the first nights of the *chowkidar*'s car-washing duty, my father looked out of the window at the appointed time and was pleased to see him washing the car.

We did not have sleeping-*chowkidar* issues anymore. Everyone was happy.

14

Animal Stories

Trying Out a Donkey

The sounds of a donkey came from the hospital grounds across the street from our house, where the American doctors lived in a compound. One day, our friends, the donkey's owners, wanted to give him to us. The concept sounded good, initially. Of course, we were a little reluctant, considering the practicality, but our friends made us an offer we could not refuse.

"Try it. If you want to keep the donkey, there is no cost"—or something like that. It was the classic "puppy dog close." Yes, he was cute, but he was not a puppy.

So now the donkey was in our walled-in yard, and our property was not farmland. We learned a few things. The donkey enjoyed pulling out all the plants from the pots that lined the long driveway. Of course, anything he ate eventually came out the other end. I'm not sure if the gardener enjoyed the extra surprises in the yard. If you sat on the donkey, moving forward was not a guarantee. He was very charming, but if you walked around him, you had to be careful in case he kicked.

We appreciated watching the donkey for about one day and then returned him to his rightful owner. I still smile thinking about him.

An Emergency Call to School

I was in one of my high school classes at LAS, and the office gave me a message to take an important phone call. On the phone was our cook, who said that I needed to come home at once and that he would explain everything after I arrived.

I excused myself from class and rushed home on my Honda motorbike, concerned that something might have happened to my family or the house.

I got home and saw our cook, who took care of a lot of things around the house, standing in the middle of the front yard next to our parrot Coco's cage. I noticed that the cage door was open. He apologized while explaining that he had taken the cage outside to clean it. Once the door to the cage was open, Coco had flown up to the top of a tree across the street. The tree was on the border of the United Christian Hospital's grounds, right by the compound of the doctors who had the donkey.

Coco was familiar with my voice and often imitated it. When we had breakfast in the morning, he enjoyed eating the top portion of a hard-boiled egg that I shared with him. Beatrice had helped raise the bird from the beginning; he had needed hand feeding for his first several weeks.

Anyway, he had never flown that high before—some thirty feet—so I had to climb up the tree. Near the top I stretched my arm until Coco could walk onto my hand and then ride on my shoulder as I climbed down. I put the parrot back in his cage and probably returned to school that day.

By the way, when we left Pakistan in 1973, we gave my parrot to a German family. About twenty years later, we heard from some friends in Germany that the parrot was healthy and had been living in Germany all those years. By now I am sure he has picked up several German words.

THE TURKEY

One day, while my *oma* was visiting from Berlin for a couple of months, a turkey wandered through our open gate and up the driveway to the living-room window and looked in. My *oma* was amused and came out to greet the turkey. She was very good with animals; she had two pet turtles in her apartment at home, and she sometimes walked dogs for their owners.

She decided to sort of adopt the turkey, who then stayed with us for a while in the yard and in the back shed for shelter. The turkey would walk up to the VW and, seeing its reflection, peck at the hubcaps.

My father's company had an arrangement with WAPDA, the client, to be able to order some imported food items twice a year duty-free from Denmark. This included a frozen turkey for Thanksgiving. This was probably good news for our turkey, buying it more time to enjoy a life of leisure until it died of natural causes.

A LOVED DOG WITH MULTIPLE OWNERS

We adopted a dog somewhere around 1972 or so. Our cook came home one day with a skinny dog who needed some attention. He thought that this dog came from the neighborhood a few blocks away; perhaps it was an outdoor dog belonging to an American family who had moved. In any case, he was a friendly dog who needed a home. We brought him to the vet and gave him food and water, and our property became his home.

Fast-forward to 1973, when our family was getting ready to return to the States. Now, for this part of the story, I need to give credit to my ninety-one-year-old dad, who in 2013 had a great memory and a sense of humor as we talked about it. The Iranian consul's family wanted to adopt our dog. The consul was living for a few months at the Intercontinental Hotel before moving back to Iran. My mom drove to the hotel to deliver the dog. Now, keep in mind that this was the dog's first trip to the hotel, about a twenty-minute drive toward the city.

The next day, the dog showed up back at our house in Gulberg, in the Lahore suburbs, after apparently checking out of the hotel and then finding his way back to us on his own. One can only conclude that he was a smart dog who had a good sense of direction. Very impressive, especially since this was in the days before Google Maps and GPS.

My mom returned the dog to the new owners, the family of the Iranian consul. This time they provided a more secure area for the dog in a courtyard of the hotel.

The last we heard was that the dog moved to Iran with the consul. I'm sure the paperwork was not a problem for the diplomats. After that, we did not have any more information. What we do know is that all those who had the pleasure of taking care of the dog were as lucky as the dog.

Me with Coco.

Beatrice with our adopted dog, Poo-Poo.

15

A Tribute to Jalal, Our Cook

I'LL ALWAYS REMEMBER OUR COOK, Jalal. When my mom first hired him, he was the bearer, cleaning inside the house and serving the meals. The cook at that time, Solomon, did the cooking as well as some driving for us. There was some friction between Solomon and Jalal, and we discovered that when the cook would shop for groceries in the market, it would cost more than when my mom did the shopping. Somehow, the change never added up.

Well, my mom decided it was better to have one trustworthy servant in the house, so she promoted Jalal to cook. She then taught him several dishes, and he worked for us for the next five years. He and his family lived in the servant quarters attached to the house, so they got free room and board plus the higher salary for the position of cook. We didn't need a driver anymore, as we became more comfortable driving ourselves in Lahore. Jalal took care of everything inside the house and occasionally got his hands dirty outside if needed, such as with the parrot story earlier.

Here is a brief story of the day that our cook came to the rescue. I heard this story from Jalal and my mom right after coming home and wondering why Jalal was in the front yard hosing himself down.

A British lady had been walking with her kid on the street in front of our house, across from the hospital. The sewer cover had been moved or was somehow missing that day; perhaps someone had taken it for scrap metal. Well, they did not see the hole, and the kid fell into the drain sewer. Our gardener may not have been there that day, but our cook heard the cries for help from outside our gate. He ran outside and climbed into the sewer to fish the kid out. The kid was fine, and the lady was very thankful, so they continued their walk. Jalal was just finishing cleaning up when I came home. It was disturbing to hear that something like this could happen, but we were thankful that Jalal had responded quickly to help. Shortly afterward, the sewer cover was replaced.

After leaving Pakistan in 1973, my parents returned after eleven years for a two-year contract. Of course, they rehired Jalal, a good cook and—more important—a great person.

16

On the Entertainment Side of Life in Lahore

DURING OUR STAY BETWEEN 1968 and 1973, we enjoyed a variety of activities. Occasionally, traveling shows sponsored by the U.S. Information Service (USIS) or the German Cultural Center would add an international dimension to life in Lahore. For example, the National Chinese Circus and the Acrobats of the People's Republic of China arrived in town on their world tour. Our German friends would let us know about upcoming events, so getting tickets was no problem.

Shows would include classical musicians, and one year a professional magician performed close-up illusions with background music. Since I was then having some fun with magic myself, it was kind of a reality check when I saw the true professionals at their craft, but it was also inspirational. It was fun joining my parents to meet the artists at the after-show cocktail party.

One year the French sponsored a well-known actor and mime, Marcel Marceau, to do a show. Unfortunately, as the show began, the power went out. One of our German friends who owned a Land Rover saved the show by parking so that the headlights provided stage lights. Marceau was able to continue the show.

The young German couple who owned the Land Rover provided great entertainment just telling about their adventurous drives. They outfitted their rig as a sort of mini-camper, with everything they needed to make the drive from Europe to Lahore—no small feat. They had a speaker on top so, in lieu of the horn, when they needed to clear traffic, they could shout out in German, "*Weg frei machen!*" ("Get out of the way!"). On one transcontinental trip (sometime in the early 1970s), as they made their way through southeastern Iran, strong winds turned the vehicle over. They were in the middle of nowhere, but they somehow got back on the road and drove the remaining one thousand miles at about twenty-five miles per hour, until they could make the necessary repairs back home in Lahore.

Talking about road trips, the big news one year was when the car rally was passing through Lahore, a race that took drivers and their mechanic–backup drivers from Europe to India. The *Pakistan Times* and the people in Lahore followed closely as the sports cars made their way through. For American teenagers in Lahore, there were plenty of opportunities for entertainment if they took advantage of it.

Other forms of amusement included enjoying performers do a small show on your front lawn, such as the snake charmers, the monkey *wallah*,[2] and one of our very favorites, the bird *wallah*, who visited a few times over the years. This showman was an older person who had entertained foreigners for years, walking with his carefully bundled props and birds to the next front lawn show. Just watching him

---

2   A *wallah* is a person associated with a particular work or who performs a specific duty or service.

unpack and pack up afterward was something special. He would do a card trick and have the parrot pick out the right card from those spread out on the blanket. A pigeon turned the crank of an old wagon truck and then pushed the cart in a circle with the parrot sitting on it. A small bird would retrieve a coin the *wallah* had placed on the forehead of one of the audience members. Before I left Pakistan, I wanted to capture some footage of the bird show on Super 8 film. So, I got the word out to find him, and he showed up. I explained through the translator, our cook, that I wanted to film the whole show. I got various shots: him walking up to our gate, a view from our roof, close-ups of the show, and then him walking away down the street. Later, back in the States, I got editing equipment and spliced the film together into a five- or six-minute mini-film, which I included with other Super 8 images of Lahore. For background I used some sitar music and enjoyed showing the twenty-minute completed film to friends back home.

The most frequent vendors that visited our house were the carpet and brass *wallah*s, and many of those purchases I still enjoy in my house, since my mom had plenty to give away.

Over the years, I saw three different student rock bands form and play at the bigger parties or events. Considering the small size of our school, we were fortunate to have some very good talent playing the current tunes.

Movies were another inexpensive thing to enjoy, and we typically went with a group of friends to the local cinema in downtown Lahore. We normally had box seats, and my favorite snack was a bag of English-style chips, which were either crispy or sometimes stale but worth the risk for a couple of rupees. Dramatic and spectacular ads in the newspaper provided several choices of American movies that the government allowed to be shown at that time, including:

A Fistful of Dollars, with Clint Eastwood
The Good, the Bad and the Ugly, with Clint Eastwood

It's a Mad Mad Mad Mad World
The Guns of Navarone
The Great Escape
Romeo and Juliet
Those Magnificent Men in Their Flying Machines

Periodically, Lahore would be the site of the national horse and cattle show, a major event with performances that included the art of tent pegging by a rider on his horse at full gallop, motorcycle stunts, and acrobats. The year I saw this show, Prime Minister Zulfikar Ali Bhutto arrived and waved to the crowd.

A benefit with our small school was that it was easy to participate in any sports team that you wanted, because more players were typically needed. Since basketball was popular, you still needed to show proficiency to earn court time. We would play on an outdoor concrete court against other local Pakistani schools whose teams had a very fast-running game. We adjusted by switching to zone defense. The big draw was the yearly tournaments between other American international schools in the region, such as Karachi, Islamabad, Kabul, and even New Delhi. The trip to India for basketball included taking buses across the border and an all-night train ride with the team. Our host teams showed us around the city, and touring the sites became a main part of the trip. Most of us picked up some colorful tie-dyed shirts and those classic, comfortable leather sandals.

By my junior year, I had earned plenty of court time, based on my height and my focus on rebounds. Some of the bigger schools had more athletes to choose from and had indoor wooden courts. Although our school was on the small size, sometimes we had players who joined us from large stateside schools when their parents were transferred to Lahore. A few players who had played in state competitions and were great ball handlers and shooters enabled our team to compete very well.

However, the games themselves were just one aspect at the tournaments. As the visiting team, we took a train or flew, depending on the location. A unique aspect was that we stayed with host families, and after an intense game on the court, we went to parties and became friends with our competitors. Our hosts might be families working in Pakistan for a wide range of private companies, for the U.S. Agency for International Development (USAID), or for USIS; or they could be diplomatic or military families.

After playing basketball all through high school, I never thought that someday in the future, after starting a family, I would end up playing full-court basketball on "Dad's BBall Night" or at my sports center through my mid-fifties. Not only did I continue to get my share of rebounds, but my shooting got better. Funny thing: By the time my high school sons Tom and Ricky joined me on the court in these pickup games, it was clear that they were much better ball handlers and shooters. They, of course, had to compete in much larger public schools, compared to my overseas private school.

Bird wallah.

Snake wallah.

Rally cars in Kabul, heading east around the world.

Monkey and goat wallah *show on the front lawn.*

17

The India-Pakistan War in November and December 1971

I WAS A SIXTEEN-YEAR-OLD JUNIOR at LAS when rumors of war with India developed, and Americans and other foreigners made plans to flee the country—or at least to leave Lahore, since it was too close to the Indian border. Once flying out from Pakistan was no longer possible, people took buses to Kabul to fly back to the States or to other locations, depending on their family's work situation. Some went to Teheran or Beirut, safe places back then.

Not knowing at the time how long the war would last, we first drove up to Tarbela Dam, about two hours past Islamabad, to stay at the rest house that engineers used when visiting the project site. My father was working on this project mostly from the offices in Lahore, but he also visited the site frequently.

Once we were safe, a decision needed to be made: Would I stay in Pakistan or fly back to the States to continue school back in the suburbs of Chicago? My father planned on staying, along with my mom and sister, to continue his work in Pakistan. If I returned to the States in December, I visualized going through Germany, visiting relatives and friends and doing some skiing in the Alps. Then I would also be seeing old friends back home, since it was arranged that I would stay with them.

During this time in Tarbela, one event really put things in perspective: My father had to go to the office in Lahore for a couple of days. His return to Tarbela was delayed a day or two. Then we heard that Indian fighter jets were shooting one of the main bridges outside Lahore, leading to the main road to Islamabad on the way to the Tarbela project site on the Indus River. We did not receive any phone calls from my father; we had only the news that a car had been hit. After we waited a day or so, my father finally arrived safely. We were so thankful.

For driving at night at the project site, the military had strict orders to cover the headlights with cardboard, allowing only a small slit, just enough to provide about fifteen feet of light in front of the car. All the lights on the project were off at night to avoid attracting enemy jets. One evening I was driving at night, since my parents had enjoyed a great meal and some wine at the Italian restaurant sponsored by one of the construction contractors. I had to drive slowly past armed military checkpoints, and I felt proud that my parents had given me the responsibility to drive us back to the rest house.

Then came the big decision: Do I leave via Kabul to the States, or do I stay? The last bus to Kabul was leaving the next morning, and I was inclined to stay with my family with hopes of finishing at the same school. (Many other students moved more often and changed schools due to their parents' contracts.) Then the news of a cease-fire arrived;

the war had lasted only a few weeks. I'm glad I returned to LAS in January, although the classes were now even smaller. I would be able to finish at the same high school the following year.

My father at the Tarbela Dam.

Me at the Tarbela Dam wearing a military jacket from a Kabul flea market.

Tarbela construction workers on a break.

The Taxila archaeology site (second to fifth centuries) along the Silk Road between Rawalpindi and Tarbela.

18

My 1972 Eurail Backpack Trip

IN THE SUMMER OF 1972, I enjoyed traveling for home leave through Europe with two of my high school friends with a two-month Eurail pass and the book *Europe on 5 Dollars a Day*. The train ticket cost only $200, and it gave you standard seating (not reserved) on almost any train to almost any country in Europe for two months. It was amazing. You could get out in a city, and when you were ready to go to the next stop, you simply caught the next train.

Unfortunately, as we three teenagers walked across the tarmac to the plane, with our families waving us off at the Lahore airport, we realized that we had walked to the wrong plane. We were slightly embarrassed as we made our way to the second plane to start our trip.

Traveling in southern Europe, such as Italy, Spain, and Portugal, we often were able to stick to five dollars a day for lodging and food.

We mostly stayed at private *pensions.*[3] Buying rolls of film or tickets to a museum would render us over budget. Before we left, my father had told me the following story about a son who sent a telex home while traveling. (When you sent a telex, you paid by the word.) "No mon, no fun, your son." The reply was "too bad, how sad, your dad." In northern Europe, such as Germany, where it was more expensive, I managed to stay with friends and relatives, which helped to keep me within budget.

What was interesting is that my friends and I were seventeen-year-olds and had just finished our junior year in high school. The American college students we met while traveling were amazed at some of the stories of our adventures living in Pakistan. They were surprised that we were just high school students, yet we had had many more experiences. Staying in Pakistan until the end of the war gave me these additional travel opportunities, which I always appreciated.

After Europe I flew back to Chicago to spend a couple of weeks with my stateside friends before my return to Pakistan for my senior year. I even joined them on a weeklong camping trip to upper Michigan, a perfect finish to my summer adventures.

---

3   A *pension* is a French term for room and board in a guesthouse or a boarding-house.

19

Brass Stories

AT THE END OF MY backpack trip in Europe, I picked up a suitcase in Berlin that had been sent to me from Lahore. It included a couple of dozen brass mini-hookahs and some sheepskin vests from Kabul, along with some gifts and more clothes. I arrived at Chicago O'Hare International with my backpack, long hair, and long white Pakistani kurta shirt (perfect for the hot Chicago weather in August), and my suitcase. When customs officials opened my suitcase, they asked me to walk to a small private room, where they inspected the items. I was concerned, mainly because of the strong aroma of the sheepskin vests, which I thought they would confiscate. I had planned to take them to a cleaner and hopefully sell them.

The officials ignored the vests, and to my surprise, they unscrewed the three parts of the mini-hookahs, looked inside each one of them, and then reassembled them. They found nothing, of course. It was all about the optics. I thought it was silly, since these hookahs are just for decoration, intended as gifts from Pakistan—or maybe I would be able to sell a few of them for two or three dollars each.

I didn't sell too many of them, and I think I gave most of them away. I told everyone they were only for decoration, a sampling of Pakistani handcraft. However, this experience led me to another idea and my first business deal: selling brass to a magic shop.

While spending a few August weeks in Lombard, Illinois, I stayed with friends who had a very successful family business in restaurant supplies. It's typical in the States that everyone has a tight schedule and is busy with summer jobs and weekend activities. I put in a few part-time hours to replenish my spending money, but I had some free time, so one day I went into Chicago by train to visit Magic Inc. This shop was run by a professional magician who had been on several TV shows in the 1950s and 1960s. It was *the* place for professional magicians to visit when in town.

I've always had a lot of interests besides sports, photography, and travel, and one of my side hobbies was collecting a few magic tricks and books. At Magic Inc., while reviewing the props on the shelves, I saw an aluminum cups and balls set for this popular routine, and I noticed the price at around fifteen dollars at the time. I told the owner that I was visiting from Pakistan and asked if he would be interested in purchasing some handmade brass cup sets from Lahore. We agreed on a price of about ten dollars. I told him that I would order a few sets when I returned to Lahore during my senior year and then deliver them the following year, when I moved back to start college. I purchased one aluminum set along with some other props.

Back in Lahore I showed the cups to a brass shop near Lahore's Old City. I asked the owner if he could make them the same size but in brass and then add a small inlaid design on the side. I ordered twenty-four handmade sets from him, and it probably cost about two or three dollars for each set. The next year, I returned to the States to go to NIU in Dekalb, Illinois. On a free weekend, I went into Chicago to visit Magic Inc. I reminded the owner about the brass cups conversation of the previous year and showed him one set in the box. He was impressed and purchased twenty sets all at once. It was a win-win, my first sale in the business world. Since then I've been spending my whole career in corporate sales.

Brass shops in the Old City, Lahore.

Photo op in the Lahore market.

20

The Science Club Trip

DURING MY FIVE AND A half years in Pakistan and LAS, I had a wide range of experiences, but somehow I was not very involved in the science club until my senior year. One of the benefits at this small school was how each student could participate in different activities. My father's civil engineering projects—designing dams with Harza—provided many opportunities that I was grateful for.

As I got close to graduating and realized that I'd soon be moving back to the States in '73, I found myself signing up for the big science club trip. Besides my backpack, I brought two cameras (one for black-and-white film and one for color slides). I had often flown between Karachi and Lahore, so I looked forward to traveling to the Sindh Province by train. The expedition leader of our group of around ten students was our superintendent and science club teacher, along with another science teacher and math teacher.

As the train pulled out of Lahore heading south, I was sitting in third class, enjoying all the sights and sounds offered up by Pakistan Western Railways (PWR). I knew that this was the way to complete my adventure in Pakistan.

At one interim stop at a regional rail station, while waiting for the next train, we rested a few hours until early morning. Before we continued, I took a few photos, and I noticed that the locals looked at us with much curiosity, since this place was much more remote than the more international scene in Lahore.

At the final stop by rail, we were met by some Land Rovers, courtesy of Energoinvest Engineers (a Yugoslavian company from Sarajevo, a WAPDA contractor). They also provided accommodations for the next few days at their rest house. It felt like an oasis, since it was located along farmland with groves of trees. This was our base camp for our day excursions and new discoveries in the desert surroundings. As we began to explore, I realized that each excursion was a significant destination, worthy of a trip all by itself. Here are some highlights:

ROHRI HILLS

We climbed out of the Land Rovers and began walking up a small hill to a plateau with rocks scattered around. Not much plant life at all. The science teachers explained that we were looking for ancient flint tools. As we walked, we found clusters of flint axes, flaked tools, blades, and cores (leftovers from making blades), possibly from the Stone Age.

KOT DIJI

Here we found various pieces of pottery from vessels as well as bangles, also thousands of years old. We walked around rocky mounds nearby to another major historical find. We learned to look for rocks that held ancient marine fossils. Learning that this had been an ancient seabed millions of years ago captured my interest. Later in college, although I was a business major, I took electives such as oceanography and geology.[4]

Nearby were sand dunes, which offered some of us amusement to climb and then roll down. We also visited the Kot Diji Fort from the eighteenth century. I was struck that we were the only visitors; there was no ticket booth at the entrance and perhaps only one guardsman. We were walking around the inside of the fort as though we had first discovered it.

Back at the rest house, we had an opportunity to hydrate and rest before our next outing. A few of us walked around the rich farmland, taking in the lush green vegetation and fresh clean air. In the evening we socialized and listened to music.

MOHENJO-DARO

To get to our next destination, we took a short train ride and then horse-drawn carts to one of the world's earliest great civilizations, the Indus Valley civilization. We ate a picnic lunch under a tree in front of the small modern museum. We were the only visitors at the time, and we walked through streets in the excavation sites. In this planned city from 2500 BCE, we saw sophisticated sewer and water infrastructure, public baths, and remains of buildings.

---

4   A few years later at college, I showed my geology professor my marine fossil findings. He asked if he could cut the stone and look inside. When I returned to class, he showed me the two pieces, with the polished sides showing off the ancient marine microfossils. The Geology Department had a museum, so I donated one of the fossils as a small contribution.

By the end of the trip, I appreciated how we had seen ancient cultures as well as evidence of ancient seas. It was a grand trip on several levels.

I recall one event I'll never forget. During the long overnight train ride back to Lahore, I was awakened from a light sleep as the train was rolling slowly out of a town. We heard chanting from a crowd of people. A few of them were marching along, swinging something around them or against them. It turned out that this was a religious sect practicing self-flagellation. It all seemed kind of surreal, passing by in the night, catching a glimpse of the crowd in the dim lights near the tracks. I was glad when the train was well past this scene, and eventually we rolled back into Lahore. Back at LAS we reviewed and labeled our findings with much interest.

A train station on the way to the Sindh Province, south of Lahore,
for the annual science club trip.

Two more shots I took at the train station on the way to the Sindh Province.

*Me taking a break with members of the
science club near a rest house.*

A local farmer.

An irrigation system on a farm.

Water buffalo along a canal.

A fast-moving donkey.

A "cool" way to travel, via canal.

A tonga ride pit stop. (The wheel rim broke.)

Hay wagons near Mohenjo-daro.

Excavated ruins at Mohenjo-daro.

Lunch with the science club at Mohenjo-daro.

Members of the science club reviewing our findings.

En route to our next excursion.

*A map of the Indus Valley civilization at the
Mohenjo-daro visitor center/museum.*

Flint tools we discovered on our science club trip.

Ancient sea fossils we also discovered on our trip.

Kot Diji Fort.

21

The Senior Class Non-Trip and Then Off to Europe and the States

TYPICALLY, THE SENIOR CLASS OF about twenty to thirty students would take a big regional trip, such as to New Delhi, India. However, our graduating class was smaller—only nine of us—since several students had left the country during the short war with India. Two in our class were Pakistani students, and we realized that it would be an issue at the border to arrange a trip to India at that time.

Most of us had already visited many areas around Pakistan and would be heading to the States to start college, many at the top schools. We all had one thing in common: We were going to miss our home of Lahore and one another, so we just planned two days of our favorite local activities that we could all do together. It must have been the least expensive senior trip ever held at LAS.

Each day we met at my house, then off we went to do a round of golf. We ate lunch at our favorite Chinese restaurant. We listened to some music, and then off we went to the cinema house for a movie. It was the best way to end our senior year, before we all packed up and left for our summer trips and college.

I did another backpack trip with two friends, starting out in Teheran, then on to Athens and continuing to Austria and Germany, again visiting friends and relatives in Munich and Berlin. Following my trip through Europe the preceding year, this new trip was a great way to celebrate high school graduation before moving home after five and a half years overseas.

Then it was off to Chicago and the short drive to Dekalb, Illinois, to start college at NIU in the fall of 1973. On a side note: As I began my freshman year, I finally got to go to my first big rock concert—the band Chicago—which played at the old Chicago Stadium. Their music had been one of my favorites that I'd listened to on records back in Pakistan.

Our cook, Jalal, seeing me off for my trip to Europe in 1972.

Athens, Greece, 1973.

Camping on a small island a few hours from Athens, 1973.

Me (in shorts) visiting my cousins, Tino and Gregor, in East Berlin, 1967. Their father, Manfred Borges, had a long and successful career as a stage and film actor. In 1973, on another trip to East Berlin, we visited him at a theater during one of his rehearsals.

DDR guards at the Neue Wache memorial site in East Berlin, 1973.

Checkpoint Charlie, as seen from the west side looking east, 1973.

22

It's a Small World

THIS IS LESS A STORY about Pakistan than one with a small-world theme. Long after moving back to the U.S. from Lahore and after college, starting a family, and a couple of decades of sales under my belt—and after the first big LAS reunion, in 1992—I was calling on some new accounts and discovered a link to the past.

I had been calling on a mix of various companies and industries when I walked into a modest-size building in Wheaton, Illinois, a five-minute drive from our house. It was the headquarters of a large Christian mission, with about one thousand missionaries around the world at that time. Its international atmosphere and the conversations led me to mention my having lived in Pakistan. Little did I know that this topic gave me a passport to be introduced to the director, who, I was told, had lived in Murree in the late 1960s. Murree is in the hills north of Islamabad, about a ninety-minute drive. His father had been a missionary, so he had followed in his footsteps. The director was about the same age as I was, and it turned out that for a while, we both had been in Pakistan at about the same time.

Every year the very small Murree school had played basketball against LAS, and I recall that their players enjoyed the excitement of visiting Lahore. From my perspective, having been in Murree once, I thought how nice it must be to live by the hills and to enjoy the clear air and the pine trees.

The name of the director's sister-in-law sounded familiar in our school district, and I learned that she was one of my kids' teachers in middle school. So, we decided to continue the conversation of Pakistan by having the manager, the director, his sister-in-law, and their spouses join my wife, Nancy, and me for a wonderful dinner at a local Indian restaurant.

The mission became a customer of mine for a good ten years. However, the business was less important than meeting people who had traveled in the same places during the same time period. After the big earthquake in northern Pakistan in 2005, the mission provided immediate relief support and continues to help rebuild with long-term, sustainable development projects in a difficult environment that is not risk-free.

I have learned that as you meet more people, discuss topics, and peel back the onion, you often discover interesting connections. Yes, it is a small world.

23

I Wore That?

HERE'S A SHORT TRIP DOWN memory lane about the stuff we wore that was influenced by where we lived, the weather, and what seemed cool to a teenager in those times.

I'll start by discussing wearing jeans in Lahore. Jeans were something you would have needed to bring from the States in those times: Levi's, Wrangler, or anything from Just Jeans, a store we had in Chicago back then. Of course, teenagers grow quickly, so what do you do when suddenly the jeans are too short? We gave our visiting tailor some bright-colored material and had bell-bottoms added, which just happened to be the latest fashion.

My mom occasionally hired this one tailor for projects, often for several weeks at a time. In fact, we had a room reserved, adjacent to the outdoor atrium, which we considered the sewing room.

In my junior year, the tailor made a white tuxedo for the prom, which was held at the Punjab Club. It looked good with the elegant date I had invited from the Islamabad school. Her family was Greek, and her father was probably a diplomat. Her brother escorted us to the event.

During my senior year in 1973, I asked the tailor to come up with something different. The prom was held at the Intercontinental Hotel, and it was going to be less formal that year. I wore a dark blue velvet vest (with a white shirt) and matching blue pants. It seemed cool at the time, and the style was probably influenced by the wild stuff that rock stars wore—or maybe by Elvis himself. Well, it was different.

Up in Kabul, for one of the flag football or basketball games, I picked up a military-type jacket at one of the flea markets. It was the thing to buy at the time; I don't know why, but many of the students got them. I also picked up sheepskin-lined leather moccasin-type boots, which were very comfortable during wintertime in our house, since we had only space heaters for the cool nights.

Back in Lahore, I found a leather tailor who made a brushed leather coat with long fringes and matching leather vest and pants. Adding made-to-order cowboy boots completed the *Easy Rider* effect as I rode my Honda 125. The boots were not really comfortable for walking, but they were perfect for standing around or riding my bike.

I picked up a couple of gold-braided black vests, typical Pakistani fashion, which I wore for a few of those magic shows that I did at the Halloween carnival fundraisers.

As I prepared to return to the States and begin college, I left the tux behind, since I had no plans to go to a college prom. The blue velvet outfit looked a little too crazy for suburban Chicago. The white thin kurta shirts that were so practical on a hot summer day in Lahore seemed a little out of place back in Illinois. But the leather coat from Saboohi's Boutique in Lahore was still cool to wear for years.

So fast-forward to the 1990s. My teenage daughter was getting ready for a Halloween party. Lava lamps were just making a comeback, and my leather jacket and vest with the long fringes and sheepskin-lined leather boots were repurposed. She had her mom add some colorful material for the bell-bottom look on some jeans she had outgrown. She borrowed my jacket, the boots, and a bandanna, and she showed up at the party with a sort of late-'60s, early-'70s hippie look. There is no moral of the story, except that what was once cool to wear gets relegated to the costume box eventually.

Open-water swim in Repulse Bay, Hong Kong, 2015.

Nancy and me sailing from Tahiti on our twenty-fifth anniversary, 2003.

Afterword

I RETIRED IN 2020 AND finally had some time to put this small book together. As I compiled my personal mini-stories, I was glad that I could share my slides and film negatives from fifty years ago. I was new to photography as a teenager and mainly enjoyed capturing the moment.

I had a forty-three-year career in corporate sales and raised a family near Wheaton, Illinois, with my wonderful wife, Nancy, whom I met at NIU back in 1974. She was new to travel, and as we had opportunities over the years for family trips or sales recognitions, we went on several vacations overseas. She is the perfect travel partner, since we both enjoy seeing new places, experiencing a variety of foods, and exploring both ancient and new sites. We like taking any form of transportation, whether it be train, local bus, boat, small plane, or rickshaw. We've been on trips to Europe, the Caribbean, Central America, the southern Pacific, Hong Kong, and the Philippines. On a ten-day trip to Germany in 1998, we stayed only one to two days at each stop with relatives and friends. We visited my cousins Gregor and Tino in former East Berlin and cousin Mark in Münster, family friends whom we originally met while living in Pakistan, as well as Reiner Raisch in Munich. We had a five-day first-class rail pass, quite an upgrade from my teenage backpack days, but I was still reminded how train was one of my favorite ways to travel in Europe. We look forward to planning more trips during retirement.

Our three adult children have also discovered the joys of international travel. In fact, my daughter and her husband have been living overseas in Hong Kong, teaching, traveling extensively, and raising their children. While visiting Tina and Keith in April 2015, I had arranged to join the local open-water swim club for one of their swim practices. I was preparing to do another 5K swim in Lake Michigan in September of that year, so getting some mileage during this visit was good practice. We took an hour-or-so bus ride and arrived at Repulse Bay. It turned out that on that day, it was a 2K time trial, complete with a number on your shoulder, with the event run by an Australian swim coach. The swim was past the shark net, and the course went past some of the yachts, with partygoers cheering you on. The view toward a resort along the hills offered a bonus to the swim. During the visit, we took a side trip to the Philippines to relax on an island. Seeing water buffaloes and riding in *tuk-tuks*, much like the three-wheeler rickshaws I had ridden in my youth, reminded me of our time in Lahore.

After a scuba dive with my son-in-law, one of the young dive assistants invited us to play some basketball on the outdoor concrete court a short walk from the dive boat. This was an impromptu pickup game with the teenage kids from the fishing village. The fast-running game was familiar from playing Pakistani teams over forty-five years ago. Now at sixty years old, I let others do the fast breaks while I get the rebounds and just toss the ball down the court.

One common denominator in fully enjoying the experience whether living overseas or traveling for a two-week vacation is the need to be flexible and to look forward to welcoming things that are different, rather than look for the same things as back home or to be judgmental. Once you realize that, you will discover the true enjoyment of travel. You can also appreciate being an American citizen and the opportunities we have been provided while at the same time being a good ambassador when visiting a host country, with all the sights and sounds it has to offer.

Another suggestion is to travel light and take only what you can easily carry. The most important thing is to travel with a positive attitude.

Enjoy!

About the Author

TO SAY THAT STEFAN BORGES is a product of the world is not an overstatement. Borges was born in Medellín, Colombia, on August 2, 1955, after his parents had fled East Germany. In 1959 his family immigrated to the United States after his father, Alexander, joined a civil engineering company in Chicago. A decade later, that firm brought Borges and his family overseas to Pakistan on assignment, a period of five adventurous years that this book helps to chronicle and during which time he and his family traveled around the world.

In 1973, after graduating from Pakistan's Lahore American School, young Borges returned to the U.S. to study at Northern Illinois University. During college and throughout his adult life, Borges would continue to travel—backpacking as a student through Europe; visiting his parents during their next assignment in Buenos Aires, Argentina; making overseas trips in his career as a corporate sales executive. Now, at age sixty-five, Borges has visited well over thirty countries so far, and along with his wife he continues to roam the world.